Take a trip to

AUSTRALIA

David Truby

General Editor
Henry Pluckrose

Franklin Watts
London New York Sydney Toronto

Words about Australia

aborigines
Anzac Day
Ayers Rock

'bush'

Canberra
cattle show
continent
coral

dry boat races

flying doctor
   service

golden wattle tree
Great Barrier Reef
gum trees

James Cook
joey

kangaroo
koala

life guards
   parade

Melbourne

New South Wales
Northern
   Territory

panning
pouch

Queensland

'school of the
   air'
Southern
   Hemisphere
Sydney

Franklin Watts Limited
8 Cork Street
London W1

SBN UK edition: 85166 862 3
SBN US edition: 531 00988 2
Library of Congress Catalog Card No:
80 52721

Printed in Great Britain by
Ebenezer Baylis and Son Limited, Leicester

The author and publisher would like to
thank the following for kind permission to
reproduce photographs: Australian
Information Service; Barnaby's Picture
Library; Jonathan Rutland; Zefa.

Maps by Brian and Constance Dear.

Australia has sea all around it, like an island, but is so large it is called a continent. There are long, sandy beaches, grassy farmland, mountains and much dry sandy desert and 'bush'.

Children start school when they are six. In some schools the year begins with a parade in the playground while the head teacher raises the Australian flag. The children salute the flag and sing songs.

Teachers sometimes take their classes outside for lessons so they can enjoy the sunshine. School children enjoy many outdoor sports. Cricket is very popular both in and out of school.

Many families live in bungalow-
style houses with gardens. As the
summers are long and hot, many
homes have a swimming pool in the
garden.

Swimming and surfing are also very popular. Many beaches have life guards in case people need help. Sometimes the life guards parade on the beach and demonstrate how they save people in danger.

This picture shows some
Australian stamps and money. There
are 100 cents to the Australian dollar.

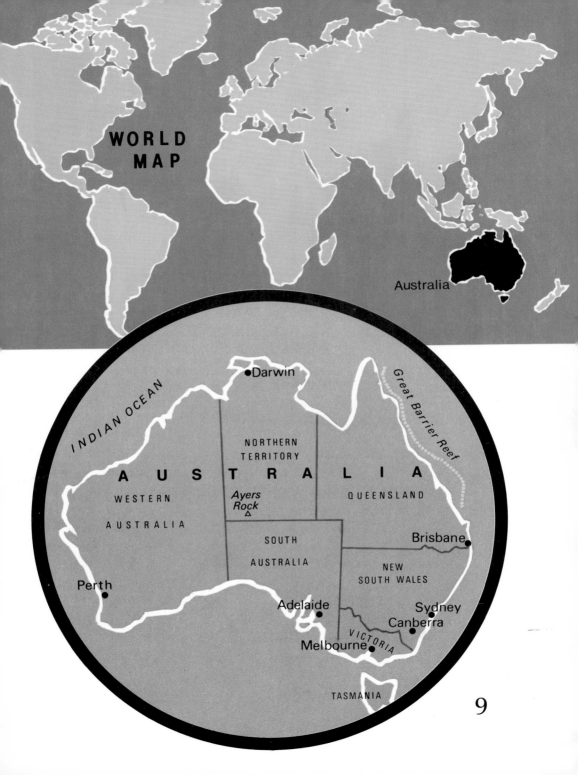

WORLD
MAP

Australia

INDIAN OCEAN

•Darwin

Great Barrier Reef

NORTHERN
TERRITORY

A U S T R A L I A

WESTERN

AUSTRALIA

Ayers
Rock
△

QUEENSLAND

SOUTH

AUSTRALIA

Brisbane •

NEW
SOUTH WALES

Perth •

Adelaide •

Sydney •
Canberra •

VICTORIA

Melbourne •

TASMANIA

9

James Cook was the captain of a ship called *The Endeavour*. In 1770 he discovered north-east Australia. His old cottage in Britain was taken to pieces, shipped to Australia and rebuilt near Melbourne.

Melbourne is the second largest
city in Australia and the capital of
the State of Victoria (Australia is
divided into eight states). In the city
trams are still running, although
there are buses as well.

In Australia the winter months
are June, July and August. This is
because Australia is in the Southern
Hemisphere. Snow falls on the
mountains and people go ski-ing.

Summer is in December, January and February. Many Christmas parties are held out of doors.

Kangaroos live in the 'bush' area of Australia. The mother kangaroo carries her baby, called a 'joey', in a pouch. Using their long back legs, kangaroos can reach speeds of up to 22 km (14 miles) an hour.

Koalas live in the gum trees
of eastern Australia, from which
they rarely climb down. Koala
babies also live in their mother's
pouch for six months. When the
baby gets too big for the pouch it
rides on its mother's back.

During the hot summer the sun dries vast areas of bush and forest. The tops of trees sometimes catch alight from the heat and the flames spread very quickly. Firemen and volunteers work day and night to put out the flames.

The golden wattle tree is found all over Australia. The golden wattle is the floral emblem of Australia. People use wood from the wattle to make furniture.

Sydney is the capital of New South Wales and the largest city in Australia. This unusual-looking building is the Sydney Opera House, which is built on the harbour.

The harbour is spanned by
Sydney Harbour Bridge. People can
also use ferries to cross the harbour.
As well as many cargo ships, the
harbour is often dotted with lots of
small sailing boats.

New South Wales is famous for sheep farming. Sheep were first taken to Australia by settlers in 1788. Now there are more than 150 million sheep. The stockmen round up the sheep on horseback.

Cattle raising is also very important. Some cattle are raised on the dry northern plains and taken to the rich pastures in the south for fattening. Sometimes there are cattle shows. The farmers of the best cattle win prizes.

The Great Barrier Reef is a series of coral islands just off the coast of Queensland. It is a good place for holidays. People can go swimming, water ski-ing, sailing or surfing. Surfers use long boards to ride on the surface of the waves.

Coral is formed from the skeletons of tiny animals. Coral comes in all kinds of unusual shapes. Diving is popular as there are many kinds of beautiful and unusual fish.

The Northern Territory is very
hot and dry, and not many people
live there. It is so hot in the summer
that the rivers dry up. The people
hold 'dry boat races'. They dress up
as boats and race along the dusty
river bed.

Also in the Northern Territory is a huge rock called Ayers Rock. Some people have nicknamed it the biggest pebble in the world.

Outside the towns there are many farms and homesteads. The children who live in the bush, or outback, get their education – even music lessons – from 'the school of the air'.

The lessons are given by a two-way radio so that the pupils and teacher can discuss the lesson. The children are also given homework to do which they send through the post.

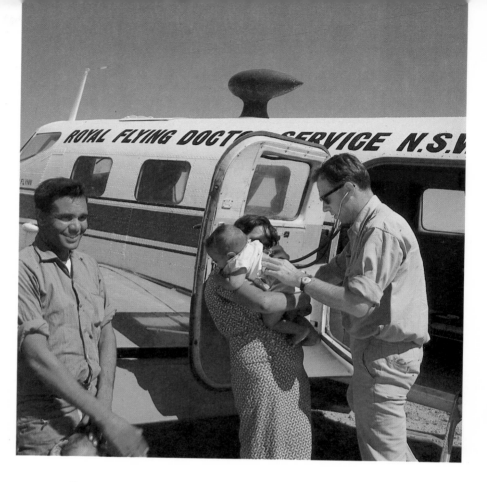

When people in the bush become ill, they radio a message to the flying doctor service. The flying doctor has a small aeroplane for visiting sick people. If necessary, the sick person is flown to a hospital.

Many years ago gold was found in Australia. People arrived from all over the world to look for the gold. Today it is still possible to find a little gold by panning it from the rivers or using metal detectors.

29

Canberra is the seat of the Australian Government. The Government makes laws for the country, although each State is allowed to make some laws of its own.

Anzac Day is held every year to remember 25 April 1915. On that day the <u>A</u>ustralia and <u>N</u>ew <u>Z</u>ealand <u>A</u>rmy <u>C</u>orps took part in an important battle during World War I.

The aborigines have been living
in Australia for thousands of years.
Today aborigine children attend
schools like other Australian
children, and their old way of life is
changing.